William Powell Ware, A. N. Rankin

Prof. Ware's $10,000 Prize Rule for the Equation of Payments

.

William Powell Ware, A. N. Rankin

Prof. Ware's $10,000 Prize Rule for the Equation of Payments

ISBN/EAN: 9783337157623

Printed in Europe, USA, Canada, Australia, Japan

Cover: Foto ©ninafisch / pixelio.de

More available books at **www.hansebooks.com**

PROF. WARE'S

$10,000

PRIZE RULE

FOR THE

Equation of Payments.

Two-thirds of the time and labor saved—requiring only one division in debit and credit accounts.

TO WHICH IS APPENDED

RANKIN'S PERPETUAL ALMANAC.

PHILADELPHIA:

CLAXTON, REMSEN & HAFFELFINGER,

624, 626 & 628 MARKET STREET.

1877.

INDEX.

PREFACE.

In presenting to the public his system of averaging accounts, the author claims as new his method of arranging the time and the computation of the interest. The time can be almost *instantly* arranged, without liability to error, thereby showing the number of months and days for which the interest must be obtained on each bill. The rate per cent. used calculating the interest is such as to enable accountants to make their own calculations *faster*, and with less liability to *error*, than it could be taken from an interest table, —thereby rendering them perfectly *independent* of tables,—by which they can become walking *libraries*, and not portable *machines*, as I have found to be the case with a great number of accountants from personal observation. Among the many multifarious and distracting duties of the counting-room none are so tedious and perplexing, and are the cause of so many misunderstandings and disputes, as that of AVERAGING ACCOUNTS.

The question naturally arises, why is this? I answer, because most of the systems now in use, are long, unwieldily, often *inaccurate*, and therefore not reliable. I would *especially* call the attention of accountants to the *immense* loss of *time* and *labor* in averaging debit and credit accounts by the ordinary methods, which require the extension of all time-bills to their maturities, the re-arrangement of the account, the getting of the number of days from one date to the other, (with numerous multiplications, and liability to error), the averaging of the debit side *first*, the credit side *next*, and then the *balance*; performing a vast amount of labor; making *three* divisions to find out *one* thing, viz: When the balance of the accounts is due.

What is the fact to be determined about a debit and credit account? Simply to ascertain when the *balance* is due. Why not go to work, *do* that and nothing *more*. By the following RULE accountants can take the most complicated accounts ever spread on a ledger, just as they stand, arranging the time with a pencil on the margin, taking a small slip of paper, writing down the interest as fast as they can make the figures, average the balance direct by one division only, thereby saving *two-thirds* of their time and labor, with *one-tenth* of the liability to error. To the experienced and critical accountant this may seem presumptuous; but for the truth of the above assertion, he, and all others interested, are respectfully referred to the following pages, by

THE AUTHOR.

GENERAL RULES

OF

EQUATION.

Start at the first of the month in which the first transaction takes place, instead of the date of the first bill. Call the first month 0, then number the following months in their regular order, setting the number in the margin, or elsewhere.

Each bill then shows at sight the time for which the interest must be obtained.

NOTE.—Compute interest at 1 per cent. per month. Any amount of dollars shows its own interest (in cents) for one month. Point off the right hand figure, and the interest is shown (in cents) for one-tenth of a month (or 3 days).

RULE.

Multiply the *whole* amount of dollars by the number of months required. Multiply one-*tenth* of the dollars by one-*third* the number of days required,* setting the products under each other until all the interest is obtained; add up the interest, annex two ciphers to the right, and divide by the footing of the bills (in dollars only); the answer will be in months and hundredths of months. Multiply the hundredths by 30 to bring it into days.

N. B.—Add the month in the margin to those in the face of the bills in all cases of unequal time.

*NOTE.—One-third of any number of days shows how many tenths are contained therein.

EXAMPLE.

24 days contain 8 tenths, 25 days 8⅓ tenths, 26 days 8⅔ tenths, 27 days 9 tenths, &c.

DEBIT AND CREDIT ACCOUNTS

OF ALL CLASSES.

(To find when the balance is due,)

RULE.

Arrange the time, commencing at the first of the month on which the *first* transaction took place, whether debit or credit. Then compute the interest on both sides of the account for the time called for in each bill; subtract the smaller amount of interest from the larger, annex two ciphers to the right of the difference in interest (read so many cents), and divide by the *balance* of the account. As many months and days as are obtained in the quotient, or answer, so long will the balance be falling due, from the cipher or starting point.

EXAMPLE.

Dr.

1871.	0, July 27, Mds. 4 mos........1350	{ 54.00 / 12.15
	4, Nov. 12, " 6 " 2531	{ 253 10 / 10.12
1872.	6, Jan. 18, " 5 " 1940	{ 213.40 / 11.64
	9 Apr. 21, Cash............1170	{ 105.20 / 8.19

$6991 \quad $667.90

Cr.

1871.	1, Aug. 9, Cash............750	{ 7.50 / 2.25
	3, Oct. 5,*Dft. 90 days 961	{ 57 66 / 1.60
1872.	9, Apr. 6, Cash............850	{ 76.50 / 1.70
	13, Aug. 15, Note 60 days.......500	{ 75.00 / 2.50

$3061 \quad $224.71

$3930

Dr. Int......667.90
Cr. Int......224.71

Balance....3930)44319.00(11.27
                30

           8.10
    11*m. 8*d. from July 1st.

Balance due June 8, 1872.

*5 days 1⅔ tenths, or ⅙ of 961.

Commence July 0. From July 1st to November 1st, is 4 months; to January, 6 months; to April, 9 months. From July to August, 1 month; to October, 3 months; to April, 9 months; to August next year, 13 months.

Read the bills:—1st, you want the interest for 4 months and 27 days; 2d, 10 months and 12 days; 3d, 11 months and 18 days; 4th, 9 and 21 days; 5th, 1 month and 9 days; 6th, 6 months and 5 days; 7th, 9 months and 6 days; 8th, 15 months and 15 days.

Now obtain the interest:—

1 month, at 1 per cent. per month, is $13.50; 4 months is four times as much, $54.00; one-tenth of a month is one-tenth of $13.50, which is $1.35; 27 days being nine-tenths, is nine times $1.35, which is $12.15; 10 months is ten times $25.31, which is $253.10; 12 days is four times $2.53=$10.12; and so on through the whole account.

Add up the interest of the Dr., then the Cr.; subtract the smaller from the larger amount, bringing down the difference, omitting the point between the dollars and cents; place a point to the right of whole amount, then add two ciphers to the right of the point, and di-

vide the difference of interest by the balance
of the account. As often as the divisor is
contained in the dividend, up to the point, so
many months you get; add one cipher and
divide, that will give you tenths of months;
add the other cipher and divide, that will
give you hundredths of months. Your answer will read 11 months and 27 hundredths
of a month. Multiply the hundredths by 30,
which will bring the time into days, 27x30
=8 days and ten one-hundredths, which is
never counted unless fifty one-hundredths or
upward. Thus the answer is 11 months and
8 days from July 1 (inclusive), 1871, balance
due June 8, 1872.

N. B.—Now comes in the regular rate per
cent. Any number of days that the balance
is paid *before* the 8th of June, the interest is
taken off at the legal rate. Any number of
days *after* the 8th of June the interest is added
at the legal rate.

EXAMPLE.

Dr.

1872. 0, Jan. 9, Mds. 6 mos . . . . .181.75* $\left\{ \begin{array}{l} 10.92 \\ .54 \end{array} \right.$

0, " 21, " " " . . . . . . .250.25 $\left\{ \begin{array}{l} 15.00 \\ 1.75 \end{array} \right.$

2, Mar. 1, " " " . . . . . . .380.50 $\left\{ \begin{array}{l} 30.48 \\ .13 \end{array} \right.$

2, " 24, " " " . . . . . . .150.10 $\left\{ \begin{array}{l} 12.00 \\ 1.20 \end{array} \right.$

3, Apr. 22, " " " . . . . . . .300.00 $\left\{ \begin{array}{l} 27.00 \\ 2.10 \\ .10 \end{array} \right.$

$1262.60 $101.22

Cr.

1872. 1, Feb. 6, Cash . . . . .150 $\left\{ \begin{array}{l} 1.50 \\ .30 \end{array} \right.$

2, Mar. 16, 30 days . . . . .200 $\left\{ \begin{array}{l} 6.00 \\ 1.07 \end{array} \right.$

2, " 27, 60 " . . . . .200 $\left\{ \begin{array}{l} 8.00 \\ 1.80 \end{array} \right.$

$550 $18.67

Bal. $712.60

Dr. Int 101.22
Cr. Int 18.67

713)8255.00(11.57
30

17.10
11m. 17d. from Jan. 1st.

Balance due Dec. 17, 1872.

* Bills containing Dollars and Cents, the cents are omitted if under fifty; and counted as one dollar if fifty or upward.

BILLS BOUGHT ON UNEQUAL TIME,
(*without credit.*)
RULE.

Compute the interest on each bill for the time called for in the several bills; add up the interest; annex two ciphers to the right of the whole amount, and divide by the footing of the bills, (the dollars only). The number of months and days obtained in the quotient, will show how long the amount will be in falling due from the 0, or starting point.

EXAMPLE.
Dr.

1871. 0, May   6, Mds. 3 mos.........$931 $\Big\{$ 27.93 / 1.86

0, "   13, " 2 "   .... 860 $\Big\{$ 17.20 / 3.44 / .29

2, July 9, " 4 "   .... 432 $\Big\{$ 25.92 / 1.29

4, Sept. 1, " 5 "   .... 384 $\Big\{$ 34.56 / .13

1872. 8, Jan. 27, " Cash......... 321 $\Big\{$ 25.68 / 2.88

$2928   141.18

2928)14118.00(4.82
11712   30

24060   24.60
23424

6360   4 *mos.* 25 *d. from May* 1.

Due Sept. 25, 1871.

Commence May 0—July, 2 months; September, 4 months; January, 8 months.

Read the bills—1st bill, 3 months, 6 days; 2d bill, 2 months, 13 days; 3d bill, 2 and 4 are 6 months, 9 days; 4th bill, 4 and 5 are 9 months, 1 day; 5th bill, 8 months, 27 days.

Compute the interest—3 months is 3 times $9.31=$27.93; 6 days is twice 93c.=$1.86; 2 months is twice $8.60=$17.20; 13 days is $4\frac{1}{3}$ times 86c., &c., &c.

N. B.—Multiply the whole amount of dollars by the number of months; one-tenth the dollars by one-third the days. .

BILLS BOUGHT ON EQUAL TIME.

RULE.

Compute the interest for the time that each bill calls for, up to the date of purchase. Add up the interest, annex two ciphers, and divide by the footing of the bills (the dollars only).

The months and days obtained in the quotient will show the average date of purchase, from the 0.

Add the time of credit (whatever it may be) to the average date, and that will show the date of maturity.

N. B.—The answer always comes in months and hundredths of months. Multiply the *hundredths* by 30, which will give the number of days.

EXAMPLE.

Dr.

1871.	0 Feb. 9,	6 mos............	$430	{ 1.29 / 7.68
	2 Apr. 13,	" "	384	{ 1.52 / .13
	5 July 6,	" "	230	{ 11.50 / .46
	5 July 21,	" "	381	{ 19.05 / 2.66
	7 Sept. 2,	" "	431	{ 30.17 / .28

$1856   74.74

    1856)7474.00(4.02
               30
          ―――
          .60   4m. 1d. from Feb. 1st.

Average date, June 1st—due 6 mos.

Read—1st bill, 9 days; 2d bill, 2 months, 13 days; 3d bill, 5 months, 6 days; 4th bill, 5 months, 21 days; 5th bill, 7 months, 2 days.

Compute the interest—9 days is 3 times 43c.; 2 months is twice $3.84; 13 days is $4\frac{1}{3}$ times 38c.; 5 months is 5 times $2.30; 6 days is twice 23; 5 months is 5 times $3.81; 21 days is 7 times 38c.; 7 months is 7 times $4.31; 2 days is $\frac{2}{3}$ of 43.

MONTHLY STATEMENTS.
RULE.

Compute the interest on each bill for the number of days that each bill calls for.

Add up the interest, annex two ciphers, and divide by the footing of the bills.

N. B.—In a monthly statement the answer will always be in hundredths of months.

EXAMPLE.

1871.	Jan.	9,......................187	.54
			2.04
"	"	10,......................681	.23
"	"	11,......................231	.69
			.15
"	"	12, ...438	1.75
"	"	18,......................217	1.30
			2.17
"	"	22,......................311	.10
"	"	24,......................221	1.76
"	"	27. 407	3.66
"	"	30, ...386	3.86
			9.99
"	"	31,............ 999	.33
		4078	23.57

4078)2857.00(.70
     30
   —————
  21.00 21 *days.*

Due January 21.

Compute the interest for 9 days, 10 days, 11 days, &c. 9 days is 3 times 18c.; 10 days is 3⅓ times 68c.; 11 days is 3⅔ times 23c.; 12 days is 4 times 43c., &c.

Balance Falling Due Prior to the First Transaction.
EXAMPLE.

N. B.—Work as before.

Dr.

1870.	0, July 4,	Mds..............$3750	{	3.75	
				1.25	
	0, " 21,	" 2000	{	14.00	
	0, " 27,	" 1850	{	16.65	
	2, Sept. 3,	" 1220	{	24.40	
				1.22	
	3, Oct. 16,	" 900	{	27.00	
				4.50	
				.30	

$9720   93.07

Cr.

1870.	4, Nov. 24,	Cash,............$500	{	20.00	
				4.00	
	5, Dec. 1,	Dft. 30 days,....... 850	{	51.00	
				.28	
1871.	8, Mar. 6,	Cash,............ 600	{	48.00	
				1.20	
	10, May 1,	Note 90 days,...... 800	{	104.00	
				.27	

$2750   228.75

Bal...........$6970

228.75—*greater interest.*
93.07—*smaller interest.*

6970)13568.00(1.94
    6970   30

    65980   28.20—1 *m.* 28*d. back of July* 1.
    62730

    32500   Balance due May 2d, 1870.

If the interest of the smaller side of the account exceeds that of the larger side, the time counts *back* from the starting point. In the above example, the smaller exceeds the larger by $135.68, throwing the balance, 1 month and 28 days, back of July 1st.

N. B.—The interest must be paid from May 2d up to the day of settlement, at the legal rate.

COMPUTATION OF INTEREST.

(For 360 *days per annum.)*

RULE.

First obtain the interest at 12 per cent. per annum for the required time; then divide the product by 12, which will give the interest at 1 per cent. per annum. Multiply this quotient by the rate per cent. required. The result will be the answer in cents.

EXAMPLE.

What is the interest on $1850 for 7 months and 27 days, at 9 per cent. per annum.

SOLUTION.

$1850 7 mos., 27 days, at 9 per cent.

```
      12950
       1665
```

12)146.15

```
      12.18
          9
```

$109 62—*Ans.*

One month is $18.50; 7 months is 7 times as much; one-tenth is $1.85; 27 days (being nine-tenths) is nine times as much.

Add up and divide the product by 12, which is $12.18, at 1 per cent. per annum; 9 per cent. is 9 times $12.18; 8 per cent. would be 8 times $12.18; 5 per cent., 5 times, &c., &c.

COMPUTATION OF INTEREST.

(*For 365 days per annum.*)

RULE.

Multiply the principal by the number of days; then add one one-tenth of the product to itself; then add one-half of the one-tenth; add up the whole amount. If 7 per cent. is required, divide the product by 6. If 6 per cent. is required, divide by 7.

☞ Point one for mills.

EXAMPLE.

What is the interest on $875 for 120 days, at 7 per cent. per annum (of 365 days)?

SOLUTION.

$875   120 days at 7 per cent.
_____

105000
10500—1 tenth.
5250—¼ of 1 tenth.
_____

6)120750
_____

$20.12.5—*Ans.*

FOR COMPUTING INTEREST

BY CANCELLATION.

EXAMPLE.

What is the interest on $180 for 2 years, 7 months, and 18 days, at 8 per cent. per annum.

SOLUTION.

3 | 180 Principal, 60
   | 316 time.
   | 120
4 | $ per cent.   2

Ans.—$37.92.0

1st.—Draw a perpendicular line, place the principal on the right, bring the years and months, to months, take ⅓ of the days and place to the right of the months, setting the time under the principal, and the rate per cent. (whatever it may be) under the time; on the left (in all cases) place 3 and 4.*

2d.—Divide with the numbers on the left, through *any* number on the right which they will divide without a remainder, cancelling each number as you use them; then multiply all the uncanceled numbers together on the right, and divide (if any) by those on the left. The answer will come in mills, if days be in the time; if no days, in cents.

3d.—If there be one over in taking the ⅓ of the days, place a 3 to the right of a decimal point; thus 2 years, 7 months, 19 days, equal 316.3; if two, place a 6; thus 1 year, 5 months, 20 days, equal 176.6—working as a whole number until done. Cut off in your answer one figure for each figure to the right of a decimal point or points.

4th.—For days only, place the principal, whole number of days, and the rate per cent. on the right, placing 3, 3 and 4 on the †left, working by rule 2d; the answer will be in mills.

* The 3 and 4 stand for the 12 months in the year.
† The 3, 3 and 4 stand for 360 days in the year.

EXAMPLE FOR DAYS.

What is the interest on $720 for 36 days at 9 per cent. per annum.

```
3 | 720
3 | 36
4 | 9
```

Ans.—$6.48.0

If the numbers will not divide, multiply all the right hand side together, and divide by the left multiplied together, the quotient will be the answer.

If fractional rates per cent. occur, bring it to an improper fraction, placing the numerator on the right, the denominator on the left, working as before.

———◆———

SHORT METHOD TO CALCULATE INTEREST.

RULE.

Multiply the principal by half the number of days; that product divided by 30 will give the answer in cents.

EXAMPLE.

What is the interest on $165 for 16 days. at 6 per cent. ?

165 dollars.
  8 half the number of days.
3.0)132.0
  —————
  .44 cents.

Divisors for Different Rates Per Cent.

Any amount multiplied by the time in days, as per example: $200 for 19 days, and divide by 72, will give you the interest at 5 per cent. per annum.

Ans. $.52.7.

At 6 per cent., as above, divide by 60
" 7 per cent., "   "   "   " 52
" 8 per cent., "   "   "   " 45
" 9 per cent., "   "   "   " 40
" 10 per cent., "   "   "   " 36
" 12 per cent., "   "   "   " 30
" 15 per cent., "   "   "   " 24
" 20 per cent., "   "   "   " 18
" 24 per cent., "   "   "   " ·15
" 40 per cent., "   "   "   " 09

COMPUTING PERCENTAGE.

To ascertain what is gained or lost by selling an ARTICLE for which a specified sum has been paid.

RULE.—Annex two ciphers to the SELLING PRICE, divide by the COST. The difference between the quotient and 100 will be the gain or loss per cent.

EXAMPLE.—Paid 5 dollars for a BOOK, and sold it for 8 dollars. What per cent. did I gain?

OPERATION—   5)800

                    1.60   *Ans.*—60 *per cent.*

EXAMPLE.—Paid 10 dollars for a hat, and sold it for 8 dollars. What per cent. did I lose?

OPERATION—   10)800

                      80
          Ans —100 *less* 80=20 *per cent.*

To ascertain what an article should be sold for, which cost a specified sum, so as to gain a proposed per cent.

RULE.—Multiply the COST by 100, with the per cent. added; cut off two figures to the right. The figures at the left will show the PRICE for which the article must be sold.

EXAMPLE.—Paid 30 cents per yard for CLOTH; for how much must I sell it so as to realize 20 per cent. profit?

OPERATION— 30—*cost.*
           120—100 *per cent added.*

           36.00   *I must sell it for* 36 *cents.*

MULTIPLICATION.

EXAMPLES.

In multiplying, it is easier to multiply by 2, 3, 4, and 5, than by 7, 8, or 9, &c.

I shall now present examples in Multiplication.

1. Multiply 428 by 15.

428×15
2140

———

6420

I place the 15 at the right of 428, and use the sign of Multiplication; but this is not necessary, from the fact that it may be placed anywhere or not written at all; this of course is left to the choice of the operator.

I first multiply by 5, placing the first product figure one place to the right; 5 times 8 is 40; then 5 times 2 equal 10, and the 4 that I carried=14, write the 4 under the 8; thus proceed: then add the two products for the answer.

2. Multiply 8844 by 14.

$$8844 \times 14$$
$$35376$$

$$123816$$

3. Multiply 64827 by 36.

$$64827 \times 36$$

194481
388962

2333772

§ Commence with 3, then multiply that product by 2, placing the first product figure in the place of units.

4. Multiply 87234 by 39.

$$87234 \times 39$$

261702
785106

3402126

THE DIAMOND OR CHAIN RULE.

1st. Draw a perpendicular line.

2d. Arrange the numbers on opposite sides of the line, as directed.

3d. Then cancel on opposite sides of this line all equal figures and numbers.

4th. If there are ciphers on both sides of the line, cancel the same number on each side.

5th. If any number on one side will divide any number on the opposite side, cancel both numbers, placing the quotient on the side of the larger number.

6th. If any two or more numbers multiplied together equal one or more numbers on the opposite side, cancel all those numbers.

7th. If any number greater than unity will divide two numbers, one on each side, without a remainder, cancel both numbers, placing the quotients on the right and left of the numbers divided.

8th. Then multiply the figures that remain on the right hand for a dividend, and those on the left for a divisor.

9th. Then divide the product of those on the right by the product of those on the left; the quotient arising from this division will be the answer.

REMARKS.

Should the divisor exceed the dividend, the answer will be a fraction.

If the numbers will not cancel, then multiply those together that are on the right for a dividend, and those on the left for a divisor. Then divide, and the quotient arising from this division, gives the answer.

This rule may be considered as a pair of scales when exactly counterpoised; for we may add or subtract, multiply or divide—in fact, may do any thing to one side, so long as we do the same to the other side; for our object will be, not to destroy the balance or equilibrium.

In this rule, also, the same principle acts as in the scales; for we take those things, the value of which we know, to ascertain the value of those which we do not know.

MULTIPLICATION OF FRACTIONS.

Place the numerators, both of the multipliers and multiplicand, on the right, and the denominators of both on the left of the line, then proceed to cancel all figures of equal value on the right and left; those uncanceled show the answer.

EXAMPLES.—1. Multiply $\frac{1}{2}$ by $\frac{3}{4}$ of $\frac{2}{3}$ of $\frac{4}{5}$ of $\frac{5}{6}$ of $\frac{6}{7}$ of $\frac{8}{9}$ of $\frac{7}{8}$ and show the answer.

$$
\begin{array}{c|c}
2 & 1 \\
4 & 3 \\
3 & 2 \\
5 & 4 \\
6 & 5 \\
7 & 6 \\
9 & 8 \\
8 & 7 \\
\end{array}
$$

——Ans. $\frac{1}{9}$

2. Multiply $\frac{1}{2}$ by $\frac{2}{3}$ of $\frac{3}{4}$ of $\frac{5}{6}$ of $\frac{6}{10}$. A. $\frac{1}{8}$.

3. Multiply $\frac{1}{3}$ of $\frac{3}{4}$ of $\frac{5}{6}$ by $\frac{6}{10}$ of $\frac{6}{8}$. A. $\frac{1}{6}$.

4. Multiply $\frac{1}{4}$ of $\frac{3}{7}$ of $\frac{7}{9}$ by $\frac{18}{20}$ of $\frac{10}{12}$. A. $\frac{1}{16}$.

5. Multiply $\frac{2}{3}$ of $\frac{3}{4}$ by $\frac{4}{5}$. A. $\frac{2}{5}$.

6. Multiply $\frac{6}{8}$ of $\frac{4}{12}$ by $\frac{7}{10}$ of $\frac{5}{14}$. A. $\frac{1}{16}$.

7. Multiply $\frac{7}{8}$ of $\frac{3}{14}$ of $\frac{8}{21}$ by $\frac{14}{15}$ of $\frac{7}{8}$ of $\frac{4}{5}$. A. $\frac{1}{18}$.

8. Multiply $\frac{1}{3}$ of $\frac{2}{6}$ of $\frac{3}{4}$ of $\frac{6}{8}$ by $\frac{1}{2}$ of $\frac{4}{12}$. A. $\frac{1}{96}$.

9. Multiply $\frac{1}{2}$ of $\frac{3}{4}$ of $\frac{2}{8}$ of $\frac{4}{5}$ by $\frac{6}{7}$ of $\frac{5}{8}$. A. $\frac{1}{28}$.

10. Multiply $\frac{2}{3}$ of $\frac{3}{4}$ of $\frac{4}{9}$ by $\frac{10}{12}$ of $\frac{6}{15}$. A. $\frac{1}{15}$.

11. Multiply $\frac{1}{3}$ of $\frac{7}{8}$ of $\frac{9}{10}$ of $\frac{3}{9}$ of $\frac{5}{7}$ by $\frac{2}{3}$. A. $\frac{1}{9}$.

12. Multiply $\frac{1}{2}$ of $\frac{2}{4}$ by $\frac{6}{8}$ of $\frac{4}{12}$ of $\frac{8}{9}$. A. $\frac{1}{18}$.

DIVISION OF FRACTIONS.

Place the numerators of the divisor on the left, and the denominators on the right, but place the dividend as in multiplication. If whole numbers are joined to a fraction, reduce as in multiplication.

PROBLEMS.

1. Divide $\frac{1}{5}$ of $\frac{6}{8}$ of $\frac{4}{7}$ by $\frac{7}{8}$ of $\frac{8}{12}$ of $\frac{6}{7}$.

5	1
8	5
7	4
7	8
8	12
6	7

$\frac{1}{7}$ Ans.

2. Divide $\frac{1}{4}$ by $\frac{1}{2}$.   A. $\frac{1}{2}$.
3. Divide $\frac{1}{2}$ by $\frac{1}{4}$.   A. 2.
4. Divide $\frac{3}{6}$ by $\frac{1}{3}$.   A. $1\frac{1}{2}$.
5. Divide $\frac{1}{5}$ by $\frac{3}{8}$.   A. $\frac{2}{3}$.
6. Divide $\frac{4}{8}$ by $\frac{2}{3}$.   A. $\frac{3}{4}$.
7. Divide $\frac{6}{8}$ by $\frac{4}{8}$.   A. $1\frac{1}{2}$.
8. Divide $\frac{4}{8}$ of $\frac{6}{7}$ by $\frac{4}{8}$ of $\frac{3}{4}$.   A. $1\frac{1}{2}$.
9. Divide $\frac{5}{6}$ of $\frac{6}{8}$ of $\frac{2}{5}$ by $\frac{3}{5}$ of $\frac{30}{32}$.   A. $\frac{4}{5}$.
10. Divide $\frac{1}{4}$ of $\frac{1}{2}$ by $\frac{1}{8}$.   A. 1.
11. Divide $\frac{1}{8}$ of $\frac{1}{2}$ by $\frac{1}{4}$.   A. $\frac{1}{4}$.
12. Divide $\frac{1}{2}$ of $\frac{1}{8}$ by $\frac{1}{4}$ of $\frac{1}{4}$.   A. 1.

13. Divide $\frac{5}{6}$ of $\frac{4}{5}$ by $\frac{2}{9}$ of 5.   A. $\frac{3}{5}$.

14. Divide $\frac{1}{2}$ ot $\frac{1}{4}$ by $\frac{4}{8}$ of 10.   A. $\frac{1}{64}$.

15. Divide $\frac{4}{5}$ of $\frac{1}{4}$ by $\frac{4}{8}$ of 12.   A. $\frac{1}{30}$.

16. Divide $\frac{1}{2}$ of 2 by $\frac{1}{4}$ of 4.   A. 1.

17. Divide $\frac{1}{4}$ of 4 by $\frac{1}{8}$ of 8.   A. 1.

18. Divide $1\frac{1}{2}$ by 4.   A. $\frac{3}{8}$.

19. Divide $2\frac{1}{2}$ by $\frac{1}{2}$ of 5.   A. 1.

20. Divide $\frac{1}{3}$ of 6 by $2\frac{2}{3}$ of 3.   A. $\frac{1}{4}$.

SAFE GUIDE IN ADDITION.

RULE.

In addition put down the whole amount until done. The left hand figure shows the amount to be carried to the next column, the right shows the answer.

EXAMPLE.

13467	34	...1st column.
46329	23	...2d "
72548	28	...3d "
9302	35	...4th "
57831	4	...last "
46357	2	... " "

245834   *Ans.*

N. B.—In the last addition put the figure in the right hand column.

CONVERSION OF STERLING MONEY.

RULE.

Place a cipher to the right of the pence, divide by 12; add the shillings, divide by 20; then add the pounds. Multiply the whole by 40, and divide the product by 9. Point off in the answer one figure for each decimal.

EXAMPLE.

How many dollars are there in £50 7s. 6d?

12)60
———
2,0)7, 5
———
50 375
40
———
9)2015000
———
$223.88.8 par value.

SOLUTION.

Multiply by 40, because in £1 there are 40 sixpences; divide by 9, because $1 is equivalent to 4s. 6d. at par. In 4s. 6d. there are 9 sixpences.

BARTER.

Place the given quantity of the commodity and the price at which it is valued, on the right of the line. Place on the left the constituents of the commodity whose value is required.

EXAMPLES.

1. How much cloth at 22 cents per yard, must be given in exchange for 4400 lbs. of cotton, at 3½ cents per pound?

$$\begin{array}{c|c} \cancel{22} & \cancel{4400} \\ 2 & 7 \\ \hline & \\ & 700 \qquad \text{Ans. 700 yds.} \end{array}$$

2. How much tea, at 64 cents per pound, must be given for 448 pounds of coffee, at 20 cents per pound? Ans. 140 lbs.

3. How much wheat at $1.25 cents per bushel, must be given for fifty bushels of rye, at 70 cents per bushel? Ans. 28 bush.

4. How many bushels of rye worth 70 cents per bushel, must I give for 28 bushels of wheat, the wheat valued at $1.25 per bushel? Ans. 50 bush.

5. How many pounds of coffee can I have in exchange for 28 lbs. of butter, valued at 21 cents per lb.; the value of the coffee is 12 cts. per lb? Ans. 49.

6. How many sheep at $4 per head, must I give for 6 cows, at $12 a piece? Ans. 18.

7. Sold 28 bushels of wheat at 75 cents per bushel; how many barrels of salt can I have in exchange at $2 per barrel? Ans. 10½.

8. How much coffee at 20 cents per pound, must I give for 120 yards of cloth, at 64 cents per yard? Ans. 384.

9. How many bushels of wheat will pay for 40 barrels of pork at $8 per barrel, when wheat is worth 80 cts. per bushel? Ans. 400 bush.

DISCOUNT.

Discount is an allowance made for prompt payment.

DISCOUNT WITHOUT TIME.

Place the sum on which the discount is to be made, and the rate per cent. on the right, and one hundred on the left.

EXAMPLE.—What is the discount on $400, at 6 per cent...................Ans. $24.

WOOD MEASURE, &c.
RULE.

Place the length, height, and width, on the right; on the left place the dimensions of one cord.

EXAMPLE.

How many cords of wood in a pile 120 feet long, 12 feet high, and 4 feet wide?

```
8 | 120      15
4 |  12       3
4 |   4      ——
```
Ans. 45 Cords.

SOLUTION.

4 equals 4; 4 into 12 three times; 8 into 120, 15 times; 3 times 15 is 45 cords.

How many cords of wood in a pile 32 feet long, 12 high, and 4 wide?

```
8 | 32       4
4 | 12       3
4 |  4      ——
```
Ans. 12 Cords.

How many yards of carpeting will it take to carpet a hall 18 by 20 feet?

```
  | 18       2
9 | 20      ——
```
Ans. 40 Yards.

NOTE.—Divide by 9, because 9 square feet make 1 square yard.

If ⅓ of 6 be 3, what will the ¼ of 20 be?

$$\begin{array}{c|c} 1 & 3 \\ 6 & 3 \\ 4 & 1 \\ & 20 \end{array}$$

Ans. 7½.

How many bricks in a wall 40 feet long, 12 feet high, and 1½ feet thick? Size of brick, 8 by 4 by 2 inches.

$$\begin{array}{c|c} 8 & 40 \\ 4 & 12 \\ 3 & 4 \\ 2 & 1728 \text{ in.} = 1 \text{ cubic ft.} \end{array}$$

Answer 17,280 *bricks.*

How many feet board measure in the floor joists of a building 18 by 40 feet, joists 3 by 8 inches, placed 16 inches apart from the centre of each?

$$\begin{array}{c|c} & 40 \\ & 18 \\ 16 & 3 \\ & 8 \end{array}$$

Answer 1080 *feet.*

How many dollars will it cost to carpet a hall 24 by 15, carpet one yard wide, at 11 shillings per yard?

$$\begin{array}{c|c} & 24 \\ 9 & 15 \\ 8 & 11 \end{array}$$

Answer $55

NAMES OF COINS.

. BRAZIL.
	D	C	M
Johannes, (half in proportion)	17	06	8
Dobraon	32	71	4
Dobra	17	30	5
Moidore, (half in proportion)	6	56	
Crusado		63	8

. ENGLAND.
Guinea, half in proportion	5	11	6
Sovereign, do	4	85	
Seven Shilling Piece	1	70	6

FRANCE.
Double Louis, coined bef. 1786	9	69	3
Louis, coined before 1786	4	84	4
Double Louis, coined since 1786	9	16	3
Louis, coined since 1786	4	58	1
Double Napoleon, or forty francs	7	71	3
Napoleon, or twenty francs	3	86	6

COLUMBIA.
Doubloons	15	53	8

MEXICO.
Doubloons, shares in proportion	15	53	8

PORTUGAL.
Dobraon	32	71	4
Dobra	17	35	6
Johannes	17	06	8
Moidore, half in proportion	6	56	
Piece of 16 testoons, or 1600 rees	2	12	5
Old Crusado of 400 rees		58	6
New Crusado of 480 rees		63	7
Millree, coined in 1755		78	

SPAIN.

D C M

Quadruple pistol, or Doubloon, 1772, double
and single, and shares in proportion......16 03 3
Doubloon, 1801.......................... .15 53 8
Pistole, 1801............................. 3 88 8
Coronilla, gold doll., or vintem, 1801... .... 98 2

U. S. AMERICA.

Eagle, coined before July 31, 1834..........10 66 8
Eagle, coined after July 31, 1834...........10 .. .
Shares in proportion.

VALUE OF FOREIGN MONEY.

CANADA, NOVA SCOTIA, &c.

A Farthing............................				4.1
4 Farthings = a penny...............			1	6$\frac{3}{4}$
12 Pence	a shilling..........		20	..
60 Pence	a dollar...........	1	..	..
20 Shillings	a pound...........	4	..	..
30 Shillings	a moidore.........	6	..	..
40 Shillings	a half Joe.........	8	..	..
50 Shillings	a Fed. Eagle.......	10	..	..

NORTHERN PARTS
ENGLAND & SCOTLAND.
LONDON, LIVERPOOL, BRISTOL, EDINBURGH, GLASGOW, &C.

			D	C	M
A Farthing			..	..	4.6
2 Farthings	= a half-penny		..	..	9¼
2 Half-pence	a penny		..	1	8½
4 Pence	a groat		..	7	4
6 Pence	a half shilling		..	11	1.1
12 Pence	a shilling		..	22	2.2
54 Pence	an Ame. dol		1	..	..
5 Shillings	a crown		1	11	1.1
20 Shillings	a pound ster		4	44	4.4
21 Shillings	an English guinea...		4	66	6.7

BREMEN.

			C	M
3 Grotes	— a double shilling..		3	2
24 Grotes	a mark		25	5¼
48 Grotes	a double mark..	..	51	1
72 Grotes or 3 marks	a rix dollar	..	76	6¼

Accounts are kept in Rix-dollars and Grotes.

HANOVER,
LUNENBURG, ZELL, &C.

			D	C	M
A Pfenning			..	..	2.7
3 Pfennings	— a dreyer		..	8	.2
8 Pfennings	a marien		..	2	1.9
12 Pfennings	a grosh		..	3	2.8
8 Groshen	a half guilden		..	26	2½
16 Groshen	a guilden		..	52	5
24 Groshen	a rix dollar		..	78	7½
32 Groshen	a double guilden	..	1	5	..
34 Groshen	a ducat		1	10	..

Accounts are kept in Rix-dollars, Groshens, and Pfennings.

EUROPE.

SOUTHERN PARTS.

PORTUGAL.

		D	C	M
A Rhea........		..		1¼
10 Reas	— a half vintin..........	..	1	1¼
20 Reas	a vintin.............	..	2	5
5 Vintins	a testoon............	..	12	5
4 Testoons	a crusad of exchange.	...	50	..
24 Vintins	a new crusado........	..	60	..
10 Testoons	a milrea...............	1	25	..
48 Testoons	a moidore..........	6	..	..
64 Testoons	a Johannes..........	8	..	.

Accounts are kept in Millreas and Reas.

FRANCE AND NAVARRE.

PARIS, LYONS, MARSEILLES, BORDEAUX, BAYONNE, &C.

		D	C	M
A Denier		..	..	0¼
3 Deniers	— a liard.............	..	..	2.3
2 Liards	a dardene...........	..	..	4.6
12 Deniers	a sol.............	..	..	9¼
20 Sols	a livre tournois......	..	18	5
60 Sols	an ecu of exchange..	..	55	5
6 Livres	an ecu or crown.....	1	11	1.1
10 Livres	a pistole...........	1	85	..
24 Livres	a Louis d'or.........	4	44	4.4

Accounts are kept in Livres, Sous, and Deniers.

SPAIN.

		D	C	M
32 Reals =	a pistole of exchange....	3	18	5
36 Reals	a pistole...............	3	72	2

Accounts are kept in Dollars, Reals, & Maravedis.

SPAIN—Continued.

GIBRALTAR, MALAGA, DENIA, &c.

Velon.

	D	C	M
A Maravedi.....,...			1.6
2 Maravedis ⚌ an ochavo........			3.2
4 Maravedis a quartil........			6.4
34 Maravedis a real velon...... ..		5	3.2
15 Reals a piastre of ex.... ..		79	6.3
512 Maravedis a pistole......... ..		77	6.3
60 Reals a pistole of ex....	3	18	5
2043 Maravedis a pistole of ex....	3	18	5
70 Reals a pistole........	3	72	2

Accounts are kept in Dollars, Reals, & Maravedis.

BARCELONA, SARAGOSSA, VALENCIA, &c.

	D	C	M
A Maravedi..........			3.9
16 Maravedis ⚌ a soldo............ ..		6	2¼
2 Soldos a rial, old plate...... ..		12	5
16 Soldos a dollar..........	1	..	..
20 Soldos a libra...............	1	25	..
24 Soldos a ducat...........	1	50	..
60 Soldos a pistole..........	3	60	..

There are also Ducats of 21 and 22 Soldos.

Accounts are kept in Dollars, Reals & Maravedis.

Note.—Although 60 Soldos are equal to 3 dollars and 75 cents, the Spanish Pistole is worth but 3 dollars and 60 cents.

ITALY.

GENOA, NOVA, CORSICA, BASTEA, &C.

		D	C	M
A Denari.............				6¾
12 Denari == a soldi..............				7.9
4 Soldi a chevalet...........			3	1.8
20 Soldi a lira...............			15	9.2
30 Soldi a testoon............			23	8¼
5 Lires a croisade...........			79	6.3
115 Soldis a pezzo of ex........			92	5.9
6 Testoons a genoine...........	1	44	4
20 Liers a pistole............	3	18	5

Accounts are kept in Liers, Soldis, and Denaris.

CHINA.

PEKIN, CANTON, &C.

		D	C	M
A Cash...........				1.4
10 Cash == a candareen..........			1	4.8
10 Candareens a mace..............			14	8
10 Mace, 1 oz. 6 dwt. 6 grs. == a tale.	1	48	..

Accounts are kept here in Tales, Mace, Candareens, and Cash.

Prof. W. POWELL WARE'S

MAGIC SQUARE.

These columns (added) make 100, forty-two different ways.

```
1 3 7 9 6 2 8 4 1 3 7 9 6 2 8 4 1 3 7 9
3 9 1 7 2 4 6 8 3 9 1 7 2 4 6 8 3 9 1 7
7 1 9 3 8 6 4 2 7 1 9 3 8 6 4 2 7 1 9 3
9 7 3 1 4 8 2 6 9 7 3 1 4 8 2 6 9 7 3 1
6 2 8 4 1 3 7 9 6 2 8 4 1 3 7 9 6 2 8 4
2 4 6 8 3 9 1 7 2 4 6 8 3 9 1 7 2 4 6 8
8 6 4 2 7 1 9 3 8 6 4 2 7 1 9 3 8 6 4 2
4 8 2 6 9 7 3 1 4 8 2 6 9 7 3 1 4 8 2 6
1 3 7 9 6 2 8 4 1 3 7 9 6 2 8 4 1 3 7 9
3 9 1 7 2 4 6 8 3 9 1 7 2 4 6 8 3 9 1 7
7 1 9 3 8 6 4 2 7 1 9 3 8 6 4 2 7 1 9 3
9 7 3 1 4 8 2 6 9 7 3 1 4 8 2 6 9 7 3 1
6 2 8 4 1 3 7 9 6 2 8 4 1 3 7 9 6 2 8 4
2 4 6 8 3 9 1 7 2 4 6 8 3 9 1 7 2 4 6 8
8 6 4 2 7 1 9 3 8 6 4 2 7 1 9 3 8 6 4 2
4 8 2 6 9 7 3 1 4 8 2 6 9 7 3 1 4 8 2 6
1 3 7 9 6 2 8 4 1 3 7 9 6 2 8 4 1 3 7 9
3 9 1 7 2 4 6 8 3 9 1 7 2 4 6 8 3 9 1 7
7 1 9 3 8 6 4 2 7 1 9 3 8 6 4 2 7 1 9 3
9 7 3 1 4 8 2 6 9 7 3 1 4 8 2 6 9 7 3 1
```

PROF. WARE'S CHALLENGE.

From N. Y. Herald, Oct. 30, 1870.

$10,000 has been deposited with Greenbaum Bros. & Co., Bankers, National Park Bank Building, by Prof. W Powell Ware, 21 West 124th Street. for the best Rule for Equation of Payments. To be decided by competent judges on December 1st, 1870.

From N. Y. Standard, Nov. 4th, 1870.

A CHANCE FOR MATHEMATICIANS. - The problem of the Equation of Payments is receiving at present the attention of the best mathematicians, an announcement having been recently made by Prof W. Powell Ware, of 21 West 124th Street of this city, that he would pay $10 000 for the best rule. The money has been deposited for the purpose with Messrs. Greenbaum Bros & Co., Bankers, National Park Bank Building. to whom competitors may send their rules. On December 1st the successful competitor will receive payment for his rule.

From N. Y. World, Nov. 13, 1870.

The mathematicians have become very enthusiastic in their race for the $10,000 offered by Prof. Ware, of this city, for the best rule for the Equation of Payments. The plans already received come from almost every section of the country, and include some very good and some very preposterous solutions. All parties interested will meet at 12 o'clock, on December 1. 1870, at the Astor House. at which time the successful competitor will receive the reward for his labor.

From N. Y. Times, Nov. 15, 1870.

EQUATION OF PAYMENTS.—Prof. Ware's offer of $10,000 for the best rule for the equation of payments has drawn out a very exciting competition between the mathematicians all over the country. The rules already received by Prof. Ware and the Messrs. Greenbum Brothers, in whose hands the money is deposited, come from every section of the country, and include some marvelous mathematical efforts. The award for the best plan will be made December 1, 1870, at the Astor House, at which place all interested parties will assemble at 12 o'clock.

Numerous extracts from different sections of the country omitted for want of space.

DECISION OF THE JUDGES.

[TRUE COPY.]

We, the undersigned committee selected to decide upon the different plans submitted in the contest for the best rule for the Equation of Payments, after mature and careful examination and test of plans offered by fifty-seven competitors (made conjointly and personally) do declare this to be our positive and final decisions, viz :

That the Rule presented by Prof. W. POWELL WARE, of New York City, is the shortest, simplest, and best, possessing the greatest utility and general adaptation, not only of the plans now before us, but of any that has ever come to our knowledge, and which in our judgment is mathematically correct.

We therefore declare that Prof. W. POWELL WARE, of New York, is duly entitled to the award offered.

SIGNED:

Jos. C. Atwood, with Landers, Frary & Clark, 53 Chambers Street.

A. O. Field, with Jordan, Marsh & Co., 184 and 186 Church Street.

John G. Huhn, with Hoover, Calhoun & Co., 302 Broadway.

Edward F. Choate, with E. R. Dibble and Co., 53 and 55 Worth Street.

B. F. Blake, with Manning, Glover & Co., 109 and 111 Worth Street.

We fully concur in the above decision—

H. E. 'Phelps, book-keeper of H. B. Claflin & Co,
John P. Gaul, with Tefft, Griswold & Kellogg. 443 and 445 Broadway
Anthou J. Kruger, with Duncan, Sherman & Co., Bankers.
Wm. H. Clark, with Henry Clewes & Co., Bankers, 32 Wall Street.
Matthew Bunker. of Benedict, Hall & Co., 134 and 136 Grand Street.

www.ingramcontent.com/pod-product-compliance
Lightning Source LLC
Chambersburg PA
CBHW021434090426
42739CB00009B/1478